The Stone that The Builder Refused:
Past Hurts, Pains and Testimony

Claudette Williams

The Stone that the Builder Refused: Past Hurts, Pains and Testimony Copyright© May 2014 by Claudette Williams

Published in the United States of America by
Gospel 4 U Publishing

Editor: Stephanie Montgomery
Unique Communications Concepts

All rights reserved. No part of this book may be reproduced or transmitted in anyway by means, electronic, mechanical, Photocopy, recording or otherwise, without prior permission of the author except as provided by USA copyright law.

Library of Congress Control Number: 2014937949

Scriptures are taken from the
King James Version unless otherwise marked.
ISBN 978-0692023518
Printed in United States of America
May 2014

Contents

Foreword..7

Acknowledgement..................................11

Introduction...13

Chapter 1..17

Chapter 2..27

Chapter 3..33

Chapter 4..37

Chapter 5..45

Chapter 6..51

Chapter 7..57

Chapter 8..63

Chapter 9..67

Chapter 10..75

Chapter 11..79

Chapter 12..83

Chapter 13..87

Chapter 14...91

Chapter 15...101

Chapter 16...117

Chapter 17...125

Chapter 18...129

Chapter 19...135

Chapter 20...141

Chapter 21...147

Chapter 22...155

Foreword

I was a very skilful football player and because of my God-given talent, my life took a unique journey. I was transferred from Kingston to Portland to play football for a prominent High School. I moved to an unknown territory as a youngster and it was during this transformation that Claudette's and my lives crossed paths in a very significant way. From the moment I met Claudette I knew she was a caterpillar just waiting to expand into a beautiful butterfly. We were strangers, but yet we still connected in a special way. Life is like a treacherous mountain - it revolts around you and takes you to places you do not want to go and will put you in difficult situations which will either break or make you. Although Claudette has been through the hot burning desert, I know that her time to shine will come.

Claudette was always poised with grace; her spirit was not easily broken. I remember when Claudette was going through a rough period and nothing seemed to be going right, but it was during that time of isolation the Lord restored her. He took Claudette's feet out of the miry clay and planted them on the soundness of mind and stability. All that she has been through has drawn her closer to her maker, who has become her ultimate source. Claudette holds on to God's word, Psalms 30-5: *Weeping may endure for a night but joy come in the morning.* Through her trials and tribulations Claudette learned to trust in God. A verse from one of her favorite songs is: "Empty and broken she came unto the Lord a vessel so unworthy and so scared with sin, but He did not dismay, He started over again and she blessed the day the good Lord did not throw her clay away".

Claudette's story is truly a testimony. Even when she was faced with challenges and had to cope with the fact that life dealt her some hard blows and it seemed like there would be no tomorrow, she bounced right back. Claudette overcame all those obstacles and now she is like rare gold.

Claudette's book <u>The Stone that the Builder Refused</u> is a heart-breaking story that will gravitate to your emotions, but it also has a lot of lessons to be learned. It is a 'stepping stone' to some of the atrocities that can be inflicted on individuals as a whole. The moral compass of it is that you stand for equal rights and justice, decency and morality because you never know how the wheel may turn.

In spite of all that Claudette has been through, her beautiful heart remains intact. The restorer of the breach did a wonderful job on her. It does not matter how you hurt her - if and when the need arises and you need her help, she will run to you with her hands open to render assistance. The enemy wanted to steal her joy but God would not allow it. I hope the readers of this book will know that they can 'go through, to come through'. Thank you Claudette for letting me in your life, when you had shut so many others out. You are a blessing and inspiration to the many lives you have touched. Paraphrasing from the good book; "The Lord is your light and salvation and you do not have to be afraid of anything".

Junior Deer
Mechanical Engineer

Acknowledgements

I want to thank God the creator of the universe, who blessed me with such a brilliant mind. Although I never graced a college and was absent more than present at school; I could turn around and impart knowledge to others, so that today they too can be a blessing to the people around them. Thank you Lord for blessing me with my two wonderful daughters Camda-Gaye and Marshana, all that I have not achieved God has allowed it in their lives and I am grateful. I want to thank; my uncle Sydney who first talked to me about the man called Christ Jesus, my aunt Sylvia, Samuel Brown - who bought me my first pair of slippers at the age of sixteen and who sees something in me that others couldn't, my brother Winston who has such a good heart and the rest of my siblings.

I miss my sister Pam and wish she were still alive. Thanks to the people of Lewis district, who the Lord sent me amongst and where many became my family - especially Ma Bev and Beryl's family. I also want to mention my two little ones whom I took in my home, Nickey and Tameka. In spite of everything, I will always be there for you. Thanks to Petrena - when times were hard you always extended your hand to help. Thanks to Noel although we've parted company. Thanks to all my friends who contributed to my life in some way.

Introduction

"The blessing of the lord makes rich and He adds no sorrows to it and I will always praise Him as long as He gives me breath knowing where He has taken me from."

I am from the rural part of Portland, which is one of the many parishes in Jamaica. A parish known for its beautiful lustrous scenery, with a lot of cultivation and friendly people. Well, my story is typical to many people like myself who have been abused by parents and step-parents, but choose to hide it because of the shame we feel. Many of us keep it bottled up inside knowing the stigma that comes with it and when you choose to talk about your experience and the cruelness which comes with emotional stress, we sometimes cannot live a purpose-driven life. We often feel sorry for ourselves, guilty and humiliated; especially when you are relating your story to some self-righteous person who feels that 'you could have done something to stop what was happening to you' - and there you are struggling with yourself. This often leads you to harbor depreciated and suicidal thoughts, which sometimes leads to other destructive behavior. Most times our family life is a shamble and this kind of wickedness drains you physically, emotionally and spiritually. I tell my story not for fame - but because I was lead to do so. For days I was contemplating what the Holy Spirit wanted me to do and I was saying to a friend of mine, "Does He want me to write a story?" Shortly after that, He gave me the name so I did exactly what He wanted me to do. It is so strange how the Lord works sometimes. When I was back in Jamaica I never felt the inspiration to write anything - but the moment I travel to a different country, that's when the zeal and desire comes from the Lord.

I was the product of a man and a woman who didn't care for me - but my Heavenly Father loves me and through it all, He was watching over me. Despite my challenges, He chose to raise me up. I was tossed and driven by the angry storms of life, but the Master of the

Sea; He heard my despairing cry and came to my rescue and now, oh how safe I am. The devil tried to kill me twice to abort the plans that God had for my life. He did not realize that I am the Lord-chosen vessel. All the tribulations and denigration that I have endured; God still gave me the strength to be an over-comer and achiever.

God is so unique in everything He does. He has a way of preparing your table before your enemies; and the very people who thought you wouldn't amount to anything, get the shock of their lives when He allows you to pass them going up the ladder - even when they start climbing before you. The God that I serve is the greatest masterpiece when it comes to transforming life. He will continue to be my refuge and strength. Without further ado, I will begin

Chapter 1

My Family Life

My family is from the poor class of society. We were what you call the 'less fortunate', the poorest of the poor. Things were really bad and we suffered. Just by looking at us you could tell. I was the second of five children; a sister before me - we were a year and some months apart, then my brother three years after - he was a sick child and did not walk until he was three. My other sister followed him three years after and my smallest sister, two years behind. We were five toddlers who could hardly help each other, raised like pigs in a pen scrambling to survive. We all have different surnames. We have our own unique look and ways in which our home back ground was terrible. We moved from place to place. I remember when we lived in some of the worst housing structures you can find. They were so shabby; the windows were batten down with zinc and our door was off the hinges more than on. There was one house we lived in where we just lifted up the door and then when it seemed like someone was watching. They realized that the door was just hanging without anything holding it. One night while sleeping, just as I was about to turn - I saw a man's hand lifting the door to come in on us. I made one scream, he dropped it and ran. Well after that incident they fixed it. Only God knows what he was going to do to us. Sometimes we had partition that separated the rooms, sometimes none. There is song that says, '*Cold ground was my bed last night and rock stone was my pillows*' and I am telling you that was our life from as early as I can remember. That's where we slept as time and years went by. Someone gave my mother a bed, so we had a bed in our room for the five of us. Later on, we got another. We all had different personalities. Back then I always stood out, basically because I talked a lot - coupled with the fact that I was tall in stature and very brilliant. I will now give you a description of my siblings. My smallest sister was very outspoken; you dare not go to her with any foolishness. We all were afraid of her - if anybody did anything to us, she was the one with the words. Things we just looked over she took seriously and she was more like my mother. I used to take care of her financially. She and our mother sold in the market and I used to supply them both with goods. She always got more on her stall and sometimes I got frustrated when no profit was generating and I had to keep putting in more resources. I would still rather have her around giving me a headache, than her not here at all. I will now give details of the last time I saw her alive. I remember clearly when she visited me for the last time. I was having a hysterectomy done on the 9th of February. She came to St. Ann the 8th and when I saw her, I said to her, "What a way me sister look nice." She had on a suit that I bought in the United States. I said to her "You start go a church yet?" She said "No". I said "You can't say you don't have clothes now", because I had given her two bags of clothes for that purpose. My children were there and they were saying that she couldn't leave her boyfriend and she got upset and said she was going. I had the operation and it was successful. While in the hospital she was sitting at my bedside and I heard her groan. I asked her what was wrong and she said she was feeling pain. I said to her, "You are at the right place, go over by outpatient." She said when she got back to Portland, she will go to the doctor. So she left on the

13th and I tried hard to persuade her to stay another week, but she said she had to go. About two days after she got home, she called to say she wasn't feeling well. She was vomiting and went to the doctor. She called me on Thursday and just as I was about to hang up the telephone, I heard clearly when the Holy Spirit said to pray - but as I was about to tell her, she hung up the phone. I did not call her back. I went in my room and prayed. I learned my lesson well that if the Holy Spirit says you are to do something, do it immediately. She called me on Friday to say that a strange thing just happened to her. She was in the market by our mother's stall and a lady started to prophesy over her life. She said the lady told her she was going to die and that the Lord had been calling her for so long, she needed to find a holy-ghost church and go so that they could pray for her. The lady gave her three Psalms - I don't remember the other two, but I know that 102 was one of them. She said to me that the funniest thing was that her neighbour had been inviting her to her crusade and that tonight was the last night. I said to her "Gone" she said "If she go home she is not going to come out back" I said to her, "Do not go up, sleep by my mother so you can get to go" and believe me, I thought everything had gone how we planned it. At about 6 o'clock she called me and I asked how the crusade was. She said she went but she did not stay, she just dropped off a bottle of olive oil. I was so upset with her and my mother; my mother was there and did not even persuade her to stay. Anyway, she said she did not sleep and read the scriptures the lady gave her the whole night. She even mentioned how good Psalms 102 was. I told her to fight, speak to the sickness and God because we serve Him and He will deliver. I told her to go back to the hospital and let them give her a food drip, because she was still not keeping anything down. We talked through the day and I thought everything was okay. She called later and my daughter answered the phone. I asked "Who is it?" she said Pam. "What did she say?" I asked, because she had put my daughter on hold. My daughter said that she said something was in her belly and she wanted to take a knife and cut it out, so I took the phone and started to redial - nothing. By this time, she was calling my big sister to tell her that I was coming. I heard the phone ringing, so I thought she was returning my call. Low and behold it was my little nephew calling and he asked, "Aunty how far are you? I asked why and he said his mother told him I was coming. I asked him where his mother was and he said she was there, but was not talking. By this time I thought she had fainted, so I told him to put me on speaker and there I was, praying my heart out. When I said '"Amen" I heard a lady's voice say, "She's gone" and the person hung up the phone. When I called back, she said she died. Can you imagine? I remember when I had stitches in my belly and some of them burst and I had to go to the doctor; I tell you it was a trying time for me, but God knows everything best. It is so sad that she isn't alive to see my accomplishment; she passed away February 27, 2010, may her soul rest in peace. Thanks be to God my brother and I were in a position to bury her. My brother played the 'father role' sometimes when the going got tough. If he went fishing for a particular fish in the river called 'mud fish' - God help us if he did not catch any, because you know that was a night without a meal. My brother starts work pretty early and he used to work at the marina when they had fishing tournaments and anywhere else he could. Every time he got his pay, he would hide it under the bed in a shoe. I found the spot and would usually take his money for a while, then I introduced it to my smallest sibling. That's when my brother started missing his money; she was taking too much, so my brother removed and it became a big joke. He then worked on a cruise ship for years. I can recall how my sister's teeth were decaying real badly in the front and every time she argued with anyone, they would tell her about it. My brother did not like that, so he let her take them out and put in dentures. That in itself was a blessing. Although he was on the ship, we were still living in one of the rundown houses. When he was on vacation, I always watched him and would laugh when he approached the gate. He would look left and right, then dash inside to make sure no one saw where he was living. After a while he built his home so that my sister and mother could live with him. My older sister became rebellious. I remember one time my step-father thumped me in my stomach in front of my mother and sister. My mother said nothing, so my sister grabbed two big stones and told me to throw them at him, but I was not that brave and all I did was cry. She ran away from home early and had her first child at a young age. He was very ill and she was scared of him. I was at a tender age and used to change and feed him. He usually urinated through his side and had to be admitted to Children's Hospital in Kingston from time to time. By that time, I was away in school and I had to leave to pick him up. The nurse thought he was my child; they had never seen anyone else visit. To this day, he sees me as his mother. My second sister and I could not get along and she hated me. I often wonder if it was because I told my mother about the molestation. Maybe she was embarrassed, but I forgive her. She was my mother's favorite, so I avoided her throughout the years. I reconciled with her after I gave my life to the Lord. I mostly cling to my brother, maybe because we were the rejected.

CHAPTER 2

BLINDED LOVE

My mother was one of those mothers with low self-esteem, who felt that she could not live without a man. Even when they had nothing to offer her, she turned a blind eye to everything that was happening around her. When it was brought to her attention, she allowed the atrociousness to continue. I later realized that she was abused by her step-father and yet still she let the generational curse continue. Instead of being alert and sensitive to her children's needs and standing up for them, it was the other way around. She mostly took sides with the oppressor against me. One day my step-father and I had an argument and she was right there. He was in my face saying a lot of expletives; he was wrong, yet still she turned on me. She told me she would put me out - even if she was present and knew that my step-father was wrong, she would still blame me. I was treated really badly by the woman who carried me for nine months in her womb. My father on the other hand was a dead beat dad and did not take care of me at all. He worked on the cruise ship for a while and did not see fit to contribute towards my life. He started working by the wharf after he left the ship. I was at boarding school and returned for the summer vacation and they were paying retroactive money. I asked him for some money, telling myself he had not given me anything - so the fact that I was in high school might change his mind, but that was not the case. He let his companion at the time collect his pay and when I asked him for money, he told me to ask Whinny because she had it. He knew very well I wasn't going to ask her, she wouldn't give it to me anyway if I did. When I did go to her, she sent me back to him. I started to curse because I was so upset. My uncle was working there at the time and when he heard me crying, he scolded me and said, "Never let me hear those words coming out of your mouth ever again" and I said "Yes sir". He was the one who gave me some money. That was the first time I actually talked to him, so after that I started to visit him. He was a Christian and always encouraged me to surrender my life to the Lord. He planted a good seed and now it germinates. He lost his sight shortly after from leukemia, but that did not dampen is spirit. He died in 2009 and when he got ill, I was in St. Ann. I was planning to see him before he died, but I knew that his wife was with him. I was curious to know what happened, because of the exemplary life he lived. She told me that after he was admitted to the hospital, she sat at his bedside and started to sing a Christian song. While she was singing, he told her that he was going to die and she was to cry, but she must not cry too much. Then she started singing again and he told her he needed some water. She went for it and by the time she came back, he passed away. I know that without a shadow of a doubt, through God's grace I will see him again. Back to my father: he allows his companion to control his finances and he never gave me the time of day, but now that I am grown, every time I visit Portland he tells everyone passing "This is my daughter." It used to annoy me so much but after I forgave him, it did not bother me. I just take it as a big joke, but he takes it even further. Throughout his lifetime I normally called him by his name. On this occasion I called him and he asked me who I was calling him by his name, so I asked him "Is not that your name?" I asked him three times but he could not answer me; he did not play his part as a father but he wants to be titled. We all have to be careful what we do in life. It will always come back to haunt us and sometimes we get upset, but we must remember - if you want good, you have to plant good seed. My father left me to the mercies. He was with this woman who had five children - his step- kids that he was supporting. My mother was about to give me to him but my step- grandfather would not allow it. I guess he has his own agenda. I am so sorry for all my afflicters; may the good Lord have mercy on them, those who are alive and those who have passed. He had three of us and never took care of us. Low and behold, he died June 27, 2011. Everything was on my cousin and I was not in a position to help bury him, so I cried unto the Lord. I fasted and did not eat the whole day or night until the following evening. I really wanted to contribute; I had forgiven him and the good Lord heard me and opened a door that enabled me to give some assistance. I know without a shadow of a doubt that my Lord is real and He does hearken unto the cry of his children. The other two children did not show up at his funeral and since I was away, none of his offspring were there. I would advise every father to take care of their children, even if you don't have money to give them, just show them love and they will appreciate it. As a child of God, I knew I had to do what was right, but as the saying goes 'the world spins on an axis which goes round and round'. The Lord was with me then and still is now.

CHAPTER 3

THE UGLY DUCKLING

As I got older I realized I was what you call the 'ugly duckling'. I was hated by everyone except my brother. I guess he could see the good in me from a tender age. I remember when we were small and they used to give us laxatives, where they gave us a bitter substance to drink to prevent us from having worms. My big sister was so afraid of the medicine, they beat her because she would not drink it. They even tried to gag her, but it was a fight. I felt so sorry for her; I would drink mine and when they were not looking I drank hers. She could depend on me. I was very soft- hearted then and still am.

My childhood was rough, terrible, awful and pathetic. It was like a can of worm were loose on me. My grandmother was a savior. Sometimes she had four children, two boys and two girls. My uncle George migrated to the United States and our hopes were high. I figured more or less our situation would be better even though poverty wasn't leaving our doors, but we were totally ignored. He did not pay us any mind - not even his mother. A few years later he was killed in the United States. We mourned his loss. My second uncle was what you call a 'dare devil'. He was not afraid of anything or anyone. He was always fighting and his life was a mess. He was in and out of prison early on and was the one who molested me. At one point he was sent to prison for seven years and I cried. My aunt was the oldest of the four. She was a nurse aid and was more stable than the others. My grandmother, who would take up for me, was told many lies about me just to get her to hate me too. By the way - she is still alive at the age of 96 when I wrote this book, still walks to the market and remembers everyone. She only recently stopped stringing her needle and reading her bible without glasses. Her eyes got so bad, I had to take her to St. Ann for cataract eye surgery on her right eye. She was seeing much better, but after many years, her eyes gradually got dim. She wanted to have the operation again but I decided I would leave it at that.

CHAPTER 4

THE TRAGEDY

My older sister and I were left alone sometimes without food while my mother was out. Over this period, my step-fathers continued to change too. I was only seven years old when I encountered my first sexual molestation by my step- father. This particular one was a short man in stature, and was much older than my mother. He was a contractor who built houses, so he would spend most of his time at the building he was working on. We were living in a one-room apartment at the time and did not have a living room area and everything else was outside. The accommodations were limited and there were so many of us in there. There was only one bed, so my siblings and I started sleeping on the floor so my mother could have the bed. My mother used to send me to his work place - he was my sister's father, so my mother would let me go to him for money and that's when the wickedness first began. He always sent me home with gifts and this made him appear to be genuine. No wonder the Lord told His prophet *'Not to accept gifts, gifts blind judgement'*, Exodus 23:8. So I was sent as often as needed and he too would tell her to let me come. I was in the middle of a mud hole and did not know it. My mother made the mistake of not doing any background checks on these men. We as parents have to be vigilant in every area of our children's lives; it does not matter who the person is - do not let down your guard. My mother broke up with him after a while. Now and then when I think back, I feel my stomach turn within me and on more than one occasion, I feel like vomiting. My step-grandfather was such a disappointment to me knowing that I looked up to him. When my uncle used to come by, he bullied us. I was literally afraid of him and would shiver by just hearing the sound of his voice. My grandfather always stood up for me and would save my dinner. He always took away my food and everyone was afraid of him, even my grandmother. One day he came by, I heard him calling my granny and he sounded angry. I said, "Granny, momma do not open the door" but she did not listen me, so as she opened it he started to beat her. I ran out of the house as fast as I could. He threw a chair to stop my stride but I ran for help. When I look back, my whole family suffered from some form of abuse in one way or the other. I pray that the Lord will remove this ancestral curse from our name and redeem us. Back to my step-grandfather who I will now call 'Papa'; he was kind to me. I always saw him as a caring person who was concerned for our welfare, but that child-molesting demon within him would not allow him to leave his stepchildren alone. He committed the ultimate sin because he molested my mother too. On one occasion I saw it with my own eyes and did not understand it then, but gradually everything comes into place. When I was near him he would let me read and tell me a lot of horror stories. He would be prepared to defend me if the need arose. My mother would leave me there, but she usually left me with our grandmother and it was then I became prey for my step-grandfather. I was molested for quite a while by both my step-father and my step grandfather - then my own uncle joined in, my mother's brother.

My uncle - whose conscience must have troubled him, did not bother me since the two times it first happened. My step-grandfather and my step-father continued this until I was 11 years old. My mother finally left him and took up with another man about twenty years her senior. Just when I thought our trouble was over, it just began. He was the devil himself. By then I was in primary school when my new step-father began to sexually molest me. We were left at home by ourselves most of the time. Our mother was always out, either she was gone to orange bush market or the wharf. I look back on those wasted years with nothing achieved and it was better she was channelling that energy in taking care of her children, because she has not accomplished anything whatsoever and has nothing to show for the years of neglect.

By then my aunt, who had a good job, came to live beside us. She was in a better position than my mother but would not help her. She would not turn the black of her eye to look at her sister, much less our plight. I know people can be cruel to each other, but when blood relatives are cruel like that it is bad - regardless of the situation, we need to be our brother and sister's keepers. My mother had too many children. My aunt was older than she was and only had two and would have food in abundance and spoiling - but she would not give any to her sister, not even for our sake. She preferred to let it rot then give it to our dogs. Sometimes I observed where she put her key and when she went to work, I took food to bring home and she never missed it. Once, someone was walking by her home and I was reading the newspaper - as I lifted my head to look, she hit me. I will never forget how I cried. She could not comprehend how I failed. Even my teachers were surprised I was doing so well, they would not understand the baggage I was carrying. The situation was wearing me down. I was sent to a new school which was about ten miles from home and I was living with my grandmother. I was always back and forth between homes and do not recall ever being in a stable home environment. During my childhood I was bounced around like a ball. Many times I walked home after school - a lot of us used to group together and do this. Although I was barefoot, I joined in. I suffered discomfort from the asphalt but that did not deter me from joining the fun. The other thing that was amusing to me was when we rode the bus sometimes. The bus came in twos' and I would hop off one bus to catch the other. I did not recognize the danger in doing this. Thanks be to God I did not get run over.

CHAPTER 5

EVIL ALWAYS PRESENT

My tribulation continued. Going through the molestation is one thing, but it becoming part of your daily life is another. What makes matters worse is that it's around you, so it seems right. On a warm beautiful day, my big sister and I were standing outside talking. My mother was out and we were alone - then came my step-father. He leaned and muttered something in my sister's ear and that's when she said "Go on Claudette". I did not frown as I went - because if my sister knew, then it could not be anything wrong, so I was at a disadvantage psychologically and emotionally. Apparently my step-father was molesting the both of us at the same time; my sister was fourteen and I was twelve. She started attending a different school and at that young age she would not come home after school. She would stay out all night and shortly after that, she became pregnant. When I look back, I realized that her young life was messed up too. Later on in life I spoke hard to her concerning the molestation. Why didn't she do something to help us smaller ones? She said she was small too. We all suffered but they do not talk about it. I respect their decision but I have to talk about it. Out of all of us, I was molested the most. I was more vulnerable than the others and I was the one who was moved around a lot. Now I know it was a cohesive plan of the enemy to destroy my life - but the God of Abraham, Isaac and Jacob is a good God. After the first interaction with my sister, the situation continued. I ran when my step-father came and this occurred mainly when my mother was at the market or when she went to Kingston. I was molested until age fourteen. I was now attending an all-age school and was doing well in my school work. I started to make friends with different students. Many of whom I was not in their class - but because I was brilliant, they would give me lunch to help them with their work. By this time my brother and I were attending the same school. We did not get much for lunch, so I would give him my money and the students would give me lunch. Then my eyes began to open after I started seeing young girls having boyfriends. I began to rebel when he came for me; I would not go, so all hell broke loose. I was now subject to physical abuse. I was chased from the yard by my step-father, who I will now call 'Shorty' - with no mother or father to stand up for me. I ran to my grandmother - by this time my step grand-father was a lesser threat. I was all over the place. We lived beside some neighbours who we were all good friends with. Especially one of their daughters and I were close and they had a brother who was much older than us. He was in his twenties, I was fourteen. I became friendly with him. He was living with his father and step-mother and we started to have an affair. I ran away from home and went to his house. I hide under his bed for days and only came out at night to bathe. Whenever he got anything to eat, he would bring it to the room and share it for the both of us. I ate mine under the bed; I did not want to cause any problems - moreover, I did not want his parents to know I was there. So right through the day I was on the floor under the bed. It was uncomfortable, but it was better than being home and that was the first time in my life I felt like someone really cared about me. While I was gone, my mother did not turn the black of her eyes to look for me. I was underage and she did not even contact the police. I could have been dead and it still did not matter. The young man told his father after a while that I was there and he told him to take me home. His dad did not want him to get in trouble because I was too young, so I returned home. No one asked me any questions, so I continued to be the outcast I was.

I slept in the bushes or under the cellar with the young man. I only stopped when my classmates learned I was having an affair with some older man. It was on everyone's plate for lunch and I could not deal with it, so I ended the relationship. I was still not going to school, so my friend Glen would let me know what was happening at school.

I was home not going to school, so I went to my grandmother's house, but it wasn't stable either. My step-grandfather constantly got drunk and when he came home from the bar, he would fight my grandmother. I remember this particular day, my step-grandfather was out drinking the whole day. When he finally reached the house he was so drunk, as he stepped into the house he started to quarrel as usual. My grandmother asked him why he was behaving like that. He wanted to know who told her to question him and he started beating her. My grandmother took a frying pan, hit him once and knocked him out. Those days were scary, I was so afraid; I did not want my grandmother to get hurt. From when she hit him that last time, he never raised his hand to her again. The Lord is a good God and He is merciful. He kept me sober through all these trials.

CHAPTER 6

A TRAUMATIZED LIFE

My grandmother began to let me take loads to the market. They were so heavy, most times I could feel the pain in my neck and I was literally straining. Now that I am mature, I realize it was only the mercy of God that was keeping me through the trauma that was taking place. I used to have to wake up early to go to the market before daylight. I didn't mind being early, at least I could hide from my classmates - but no matter how I tried, someone always saw me and I was the laughing stock at school. I lived in some of the most run-down homes you can think of; shacks as they were called in those days and my home was talked about by my classmates too. I was scorned most days because I smelled bad. One time I was placed in the dance group at school but my stay was cut short because I smelled so bad, they took me out. My emotion was crushed. It was not that the instructor was quiet about it; she stubbed up her nose and made the sound that goes with it to make sure everyone knew. But through it all, the Lord preserved me. I will continue with my market experience. I started to sleep at the market with my grandmother and would not go home without her. All this time, with no mother to ask about my welfare. It was a trying time for me, my only bed was the ground with some banana trash. It was very hard and made sleeping uncomfortable, but I still preferred to stay there instead of going home. While in the market, I met a lady by the name of Liz from Kingston. She usually let me help sell her goods on weekends and would give me a little money, which would help me in school about two days. I walked up and down with my bundle of scallion until I sold them off, then I would go for a new one. She let me stay more at the stall and there I was selling a wide variety of things and after a while, I began hiding money away for myself. She caught me one day and told me not to come back. I felt bad - my main hustle was gone, plus the embarrassment I faced when I tried explaining why I wasn't with Liz anymore. This now posed a problem; I did not have anyone to turn to knowing that I would be out of school. Anyway, I went and stayed where my grandmother was cooking.

During this time I had not seen my mother or my siblings for a while. You would think I was a stranger; my grandmother's house was just one house away from my mother's - yet no one came looking for me. I hurt my ankle and could hardly walk, but I decided to scramble over to my mother's to look for them. My grandmother had gone on an errand so I decide to go. Because of my stepfather I was not allowed in the house, so I remained outside and called. When I saw them, I was really glad to see them but I did not get to say much. I wasn't even there for ten minutes when Shorty showed up. I was told to leave with all sorts of expletives. I could hardly walk. I cried so hard that day, to know that I had not seen them for so long - only to be driven away like a dog. A neighbour heard the loud uproar and came to my rescue. He let me hold onto him and took me to my grandmother. My mother was there and did not say a word. She watched that man abuse me verbally and did nothing. I felt like someone stabbed me with a knife. I was so hurt and let down that even as I was writing this paragraph, I was crying so uncontrollably. If you saw me at that moment, you would wonder if something had happened to me or my children. Through this ordeal, the good Lord kept me sane and when I took a retrospective view of my life of all the things I have been through, I now know why the Lord wanted me to write this book. Too much hurt and abuse, too much bitterness, too much anger. Even when I thought it was resolved and I had forgiven all asunder, He just wanted me to get rid of the pain which really worked and helped me through the process of writing once and for all. I know through Him I will be able to achieve this objective. I just want to thank the Lord for the spirit of Joseph.

CHAPTER 7

THE PRODIGAL DAUGHTER

Someone spoke to my mother and encouraged her to take me back because I was still sleeping in the market and a lot of people were getting concerned. She took me back in. I returned home only to re-live the pain, except this time my step-father was molesting my second to last sister - she was ten years old at the time. All this time I had not said anything to anyone concerning my molestation but when I saw him, I said to myself something is wrong. I could not allow my sister to continue going through what I had gone through. I said to myself this man is sick, I have to do something. You know molestation is like anaesthetic; it makes you paralyzed, you are rendered helpless and at a disadvantage. It's like being on the operation table where the doctor is supposed to operate on your hand, but he is operating on your head instead and there is nothing you can do. My mother was not paying attention. It didn't matter what he did to us, it was alright by her; she just accepted his behavior. I tell myself they are going to regret taking me back; I am finally going to become the problem child they always presumed me to be and no matter what, I was going to talk even if I ended up back in the market. She never put up a fight, not even to say leave the child alone. I was at his mercy always.

I noticed he started taking my sister to the bush. I know that was one of his spots where he used to molest me too, so I decided everything must come to an end. The next time he took her, I was going to send my smaller sister with them. On Sunday morning, I heard him call her and say they were going to the bush. I called my sister knowing he could not refuse her coming - it would be too obvious. I told her to watch them, not to let them out of her sight. My youngest sibling was his, so he did not molest her, but my step-grandfather did. She told me a year before she died. I was so astonished that she keep it a secret all these years. I was hurt and overwhelmed because I thought she escaped the curse, but I was wrong. Back to the matter at hand. I knew that to challenge him I had to have concrete evidence. I did not want to be beaten to death for making an accusation against him that did not have any merit. So I waited patiently until my sister came, then I asked her if he bothered her. When she told me what occurred, it was so sickening I cannot tell you. I was mad. I approached my mother at the same time and told her what he did. Guess what she did? She brought him before me and said "Shorty, Claudette is say that you have been molesting Peggy" (not her real name) sarcastically. I was amazed. I did not think she would take it that lightly. Now that I am more mature, I know without a shadow of a doubt she knew before I told her. It is hard to believe she did not know. How could someone learn that their ten-year old child has been molested and take it so lightly? I thought she would have called my sister first to find out what happened. I was thinking; I finally got him, he has to leave now, then my mother will show me love. I was in for a shock. There I was in the middle - he called my sister and would you believe she denied it? I was not sure what was going to take place. My last hope was my little sister, who was his child (remember I just came back) and to be in such a predicament, I got nervous. He called my sister and asked her if he bothered Peggy. Trust me, God was on my side because she boldly said "Yes daddy". You can imagine how relieved I felt. My mother got a piece of stick and started beating my sister and when it mashed up on my sister, she hit the man with it twice. Imagine me, I cried for years for what my mother did to my sister that day. I told my brother and grandmother and this made her mad. She wanted to keep his nastiness a secret but I wasn't going to grant her that favor. Demons like that need to be exposed and expelled so they can die a natural death.

CHAPTER 8

ANOTHER CROSS TO BEAR

After this episode, my burden became harder and so my saga continued. I was stopped from going to school and my mother began showing dislike for me openly. Shorty began to spend money-buying clothes for my sisters, but nothing for my brother and me. He said we shouldn't call him daddy anymore; only my sisters should. I remember this little dress I had, it was a floral pattern of different colors. It was a blessing in disguise. If more than one function was going on at school, I would wash it then ring it out to remove the excess water so that I could wear it the following day. Life wasn't easy but I had to make the very best of it. If my smaller siblings and I quarrelled, I could hear my mother clearly telling them words to say to me; and when the fight occurred between one sister, and me the other joined in. They always fought me in pairs. My mother treated me like I was not her belly pain, but the bible says that the stone that the builder refused shall become the head corner stone. I will never forget this little old man that lived above us. I tell you that man was a blessing - many times he saved me from hunger, but everything in life comes with a price. He too had his way with me. He also passed away. At home when my mother was giving me food, she gave me the smallest amount even though I was the biggest one home. She rolled the plate on the floor before me after everyone else was served. She could not bear to call my name; she hated me with a passion. She never called me like the rest, but God will turn a situation around. It doesn't matter how bad it is or how it looks - the Lord will come through in His own timing.

I was mainly on my own, without any guidance. I did as I pleased, slept with who I felt like sleeping with and would go and come as I liked. I wasn't even thinking of disease and pregnancy at the time. It's only through the mercy of God that I am alive and not walking up and down eating out of garbage pans or snatched away in some mental institution; or put in a situation where I was not able to be a productive member of society. God would not allow my life to be wasted away. I was living by the railway station, so it was a pleasure for me to normally hop the trains in the evenings. I did not see the danger in doing so, then one evening I did not hear the horn of the train blow. When I realized the train had already passed, I picked up speed and I fell and split my knee. To this day, the mark is still evident. From that day, I stopped hopping trains and learned to take better care of myself.

With everything going on around me, my life continued to be a living hell. My mother then rubbed alcohol in the wound; she married Shorty. I was back at my grandmother's. Life was hard.

CHAPTER 9

THE CURSE IS BROKEN

It became worse for me being despised by my own flesh and blood. I was alone didn't know how to share what was happening to me, so I bore the burden. I had school friends but was scared of their mouths, so I kept everything bottled up in me for years. I was glad to put an end to the molestation; to an era of a generational curse that continued for too long. I was not loved for doing it, but God loves me because He doesn't love ugliness. I was neglected and it was pitiful to see me. When I went back to school, my uniform was in horrible condition, I was crushed. You would think I slept in my uniform while other students wore gabardine materials. The irony of it all was that I was barefoot; the only student in the entire school without shoes. Because of the outcast I had become, I sought refuge at my aunt's. While things were much better with her, my aunt wasn't any kinder. She had me eating on the floor while her children ate around the table. I slept on the floor in a crocus bag, while her children slept on the bed. After a while I could not stay because the floor was too cold, so I returned home to my mother. Being there, I was like a lost sheep without a shepherd to guide me, so I just roamed the plains of the land. My friend Glen and I go way back. We met at my all-age school, so sometimes I would go to her home and her mom would give me dinner and sometimes I slept over. In those days we had bed bugs - they were called 'chink'. I was bitten nightly, so I was glad to sleep elsewhere. But there was a rude awakening - they were at my friend's too, so we had one big laugh. All through my years of disadvantage, she was there for me. I did not tell her about the molestation because it was too embarrassing. Even when my step-father questioned her and she told me, I still did not say anything. I did not want her to look down on me. I was more afraid of my school community hearing about it, so I carried this hurt for years. I didn't say a word until I was much older. I remember the first time I tried talking about it; it was with my Uncle Sydney. I still did not tell him about myself - I told him about my sisters and how I cried that day. It takes a lot of courage to share this type of cruelness. Throughout the years I told their story until I got the courage to relate my own pain. To be honest, I never knew there was a creator, because if I did - I would wonder why He allowed a little child to suffer so much wickedness. I will continue my saga. I was still at my mother's and rarely attended school, but whenever I went - I always shined. I was just a brilliant child with no one to help or see my plight. I would go for a month, then stop going for another three months. That was how it was for a long time. My final year was approaching and it was also exam time. I wasn't around, but the Principal at the time started to inquire about me. He was told that I had not been to school for a while. He told the class that if anyone could get in touch with me - even to bring my birth certificate, I could take the ninth grade achievement test. That's when my friend Glen came and got it. She did not know my address, so she gave a wrong one, but I took the exam. When the results came, everyone passed but there wasn't a result for me at that time because of my age. I completed the same papers but for a higher school; to attend this boarding school, I had to get a 100% in all subject areas. Students at my school rarely passed to attend there. I can remember some of the teachers trying to console me: telling me I had to get everything correct - at least 100% on all the papers, so I must go easy on myself. Meanwhile, all my friends began attending their new school and I was at home. One day my mother sent me to the shop. As I walked into the shop, this man called me and asked me how old I was and I told him I was sixteen. He said, "Don't you know that you are a big girl and should not be barefoot?" I told him yes, but that I did not have any slippers. He asked if he bought shoes for me, would I take them and I told him yes. He said he was going to buy a pair and leave them with the lady at the shop for me and I thanked him. I returned Friday, the lady gave them to me and I put them on at the same time. When I got home, nobody asked how I got them, so I kept it to myself. I saw the man again after that. I had not received my exam results yet - so when he asked me why I was not in school, I told him I failed my exam. He said his wife taught at the high school where all of my friends were going and he would ask her to look into things for me. That was the school all my classmates had passed for and I was so glad. Anyway the process was taking so long, I began to get frustrated. Then I realized she wasn't interested in helping me; she could not understand why he wanted to assist me. He was just moved by compassion, but he was a man who had great respect for his wife and did not want to pressure her, for her to think otherwise. When I became an adult he would not give me his home telephone number - even though I was like his daughter, he said he couldn't afford for me to call his home because he did not want his wife to answer. He would then have to start explaining and she would not understand. I wish every man could think with that great level of respect for their wife like him. He was in an accident years after; there were three people in the car, but miraculously he was the only one that didn't die. God spared him; the good you do in life will follow you. He played a vital role in my life. He encouraged me, sent money when I was away at school - and even though he was disappointed when I got pregnant, he still believed I could achieve. He helped me to secure my first job: May the good Lord continue to bless him for the rest of his days. When I told my friend Desmond about him I had to laugh; he wanted to know if he had abused me too. I told him no, that he was just a fine gentleman who was in a better position than I, so he just helped. He was rare and one of a kind.

CHAPTER 10

GOD'S FAVOR

I had some friends near a place they called 'free school'. My friend Luther was a police officer and a tower of strength for me. He got blinded on the job, which was a sad time. He too passed away and did not get to see my achievement. He always tried to help me as well. People thought we were more than friends, but the truth was that we were like brother and sister. I did not cross the line.

With my friend's wife not delivering I was back to square one; I just walked up and down the streets. One day in October, I left home and was near Luther. The rain was falling so hard that day and while there, I heard someone calling me. When I looked, it was my big sister. She was laughing and waving and saying something. When I got closer she said, "You passed", I said pass what? She repeated, "You passed your exam". I started to scream. She took me by the hand and said come. The telegram was at another location, but when we arrived it was there. I had my result even before my peers - but because my friend gave the wrong address, (I know it wasn't intentional) it went to the wrong postal agent. When the school saw that I did not take up my placing, they sent the telegram to find out if I was still coming. I rushed to my school with the letter; it was pure joy, everyone was happy for me. Even to this day, my name is on the honor board which was installed by the Principal for all students who pass exams. You can imagine the sense of pride I felt - the joy, the gladness to know that I had finally succeeded. I knew there was a reason why I was preserved through all the atrocities that were committed against me, yet I still came out triumphant.

I left about three weeks later for boarding school. I did not have to pay any sort of school fee at the time; the package came with boarding, books and food but you had to pay for all exams, so the transition to go was easy. It was all girls, so I was happy - but after settling, I realized this in itself was a challenge. The second year students bullied me. Can you imagine? I was just getting away from my plight, only to come into this. I used to cry and the tears would flow, then I began to feel sorry for myself. They would make me 'blow out blub'; they kept their finger on the switch, so when the said blow, you had to blow and they decided the time span to flicker on and off. I would sing with the broomstick (that was your microphone and stand) before the whole school with my bag of books on my head.

They picked on me more than the rest of my classmates; but I figured more or less since I did not have any family visit, I was easy to manoeuvre. Sometimes I could be passing the kitchen and I would be called to peel a bunch of bananas, even when I was on a different duty. In those days you could never dare to be rude to your seniors. With all due credit, we were well disciplined and that's where I learned to speak English fluently. On occasions when I went home and opened my mouth, people were just amazed and would ask if I had traveled abroad. I went through some rough situations too. With no family visits, my hygiene was very bad and I was constantly talked about, which was very embarrassing. One of my classmates usually gave me her clothes and I was very grateful. That set the trend for how I am today; I will give away my last without even thinking about it. Thank you God for your favor!

CHAPTER 11

LOOKS ARE DECEIVING

There was an incident at school and on this particular day, I was outside with four students. When they left, I saw a purse on the bench and I took it. I did not ask who it belonged to and when one of the students came to look for it, I pretended like I had not seen it. She told the teachers and they called the four of us. When everything was finished, the teachers decided that the two other girls took the purse. I tell you, looks are deceiving; they thought I looked too innocent to do it and because the two other girls were always getting into trouble - it was them. So they were punished and taken out of the dormitory and put in the passage to sleep. I could not sleep that night knowing they were innocent. That was the first time I was introduced to my conscience. I couldn't keep the money. I had already discarded the purse - so I wrote the Principal, included the money in the letter and told her it was me. I told her that I wanted the money to buy roll-on and that the other students had nothing to do with it. They put me out there with them but still would not let them back in - the teachers were saying they let me do it. That was an experience for me. Even today I can't do any wickedness and I would not like to feel the way I did ever again. I tried my best not to get into any more trouble. During one of my summer holidays, I went to Kingston with one of my friends and she was in a relationship with this guy. We were both attending high school and I noticed that his other brother was there, but I did not pay that any mind. We ate and went to bed. By this time, I did not realize that the room I was in was her friend's brother's room. In the middle of the night - just as I was turning, my hand touched something. When I looked, it was the brother behind me sleeping. I tell you I had a panic attack; he could not believe he had to leave immediately and that's when I was able to calm down. She had to cut the holiday short to get me home and from that, I learned my lesson; I don't go to anyone's place unless I know who lives there.

CHAPTER 12

TRAGEDY STRIKES AGAIN

I did hair dressing at the time for my practical. I was supposed to take my exam, but due to lack of funding, I wasn't able to. The same thing happened when I was to take my CXC examinations, so I graduated with only three Jamaica school certificate passes. At the end of school, I went back home lacking in will, with no driving force behind me and no help to go to evening classes. I started walking the streets again and met this guy who was older than me. We had a brief affair and I got pregnant with my first child at age eighteen. The father accepted the pregnancy, but because my mother and I wanted to get rid of it, I told him I was not pregnant. She gave me a dose of medicine but I could only drink two of them. When I drank it - I passed out and at the end of two months, I was still pregnant. When I told the guy I was still pregnant, this time he said he was not the father because I already told him he was not. Now my trouble begins again in a different form; I was not working, things were already tough and life had handed me another blow. If someone had told me during those rough times that things were going to get better - I would have laughed them to scorn. It was like I was on the rough sea in a boat without sails and the boisterous wind and waves were just battering me to and fro. I was getting bigger without any clothes and boy it was rough. I would cry for hours. My mother had a green strapless dress and I started to wear it. I had slippers, but the bottoms of my feet were on the ground. I would still wear those slippers and nobody knew that I was practically barefoot. I told my friend Luther and he bought me a pair of shoes in my eighth month. I got some work and that was a blessing in disguise; the money from the job helped me purchase baby clothes because I didn't have any. A friend of mine was pregnant and she reassured me that she would give me some baby things, which she did. She usually helped me and was good to me, but her life was cut short; her boyfriend killed her. That too was sad. My child was born the twelfth of May, but all was not well. About two days after, his tummy was swollen and he was yellow in color. I had to bring him back to the hospital for treatment and the doctor said he had jaundice and was being transferred to Kingston. I went to look for him and that was when the doctor told me he was born without the opening in his anus. He asked if I had noticed that he was not passing any feces and said he had to have an operation. Can you imagine the guilt I felt knowing that I was drinking those things? I only told my mother - no one else knew. Many of my relatives and friends - including my two children will be in shock when they read this. I kept the secret for years and nobody would know if I had not written about it. I used to have to take him to Kingston and by then his father, who was a police officer, started to support him. He only lived for a year and six months; he passed away and that was a heartbreaking time for me. All the guilt came back and I was depressed for a while.

CHAPTER 13

MY STORMY LIFE

The man who bought my first pair of shoes for me when I was sixteen, asked me if I wanted to work when he saw what was taking place with me. I said yes and he told me he was going to ask his friend about a job for me. On the day of the interview the lady said to me, (I will never forget) "You are smelling so bad, I do not want to give you the job, but because you did so well, I am giving you a chance to clean up", I was so embarrassed. After that I started to work as a data-processing clerk but the smell was a problem; it would not leave me. My co-workers would wrinkle their noses and make sounds, so the boss had to talk to me time after time. I did not want to lose the job; so there I was trying all sort of remedies just to correct the situation. I was using different deodorants but it just would not help. Then someone told me to use baking soda with powder under my arms, so that's what I did and it helped me. I know that a lot of people suffer this embarrassment - but all you have to do is bathe properly, then mix baking soda and powder together and put it under your arms. It will let you sweat a lot - but don't mind that, gradually the smell will go away. I was able to work without further incident. I began to put myself together, so during this time I met my children's father. He was a salesman in the market and seemed to be a nice person, but there is an old saying that says 'not everything that glitters is gold' and it would only be a matter of time before history repeated itself. I was still living at home and was really glad to have somewhere to go on weekends. I was still working and he had two baby's mothers already - plus he was involved with someone else. That did not bother me, it was the norm. When I got pregnant with our first child, the other person was pregnant too. She was living with her mom. He also he moved her in after the baby was born, so I rented an apartment, so that I could have my privacy. After my child was born I returned to work when she was three months old. I usually took her to my mother's and picked her up in the evenings. My mother, may the good Lord have mercy on her soul; not long after, she was not even there for a month.

CHAPTER 14

WOLVES IN SHEEP'S CLOTHING

One day I came from work and there was my step-father holding my child in a way I did not like. I would advise mothers not to let any man - it does not matter if he is the dad or step-dad, hold your girl child with her legs apart and her face leaning on their chest with his hands around her back. I am not saying that some situations are not innocent, but you will never know until something goes wrong. By that time it will be too late and the scar would already be left. Why would anyone want to hold a child in that manner anyway? For decency's sake, close her legs and put her on your legs. I took offense right away; then to make matters worse, I heard he bathed her sometimes. I got angry and went to my mother. I said to her, "How could you let him bathe my child and look how he holds her? My younger sisters were in the kitchen with her and they both started in on me. I will never forget, how my mother sat there and told them to tell me 'that soldier man burst me up'. What made it so bad was that there was a rumor going around 'that soldier man had burst me up'. During that time I was on the streets in my area and that was a big disgrace. She knew it was a lie and yet still after four years, she threw it in my face. It did not matter; as long as I was afflicted, that was what my own mother did to me. Life is so funny. Sometimes people who have experienced what I have gone through become bitter and don't want to see their afflicters. I implore you to try and forgive them; I am not saying it's easy because I still have issues dealing with it. We just have to let it go, otherwise it will eat at us, like how the 'chichi' eat wood. The good

Lord will heal us in due process as we cry out to him. I took her that day and did not leave my child with her anymore. I left her with my landlady instead. After a while, my baby's father and his baby's mother separated - now that she was out of the picture, he said I should move in with him. That was foolish on my part, but as the saying goes 'love is blind', so I walked in with my eyes closed. Everything was copacetic for a while, then things began to change. My child's father became mean. I could not go anywhere - not even to visit my relatives and if I dared to disobey him, there was always a conflict. One day I decided to take my child to visit my aunt against all odds. First he told me to give him his keys, so I did and continued on my journey. When I returned he wouldn't open the door, so I was locked out of the house with a young child. We had to sleep in an outside kitchen on the ground. Another time, I entered a beauty contest that my company put on. He went to Kingston that day and on his way back he came to get me. I told him it was my turn to go on stage, but he wanted me to leave. I decided I would stay and compete in the contest, so he rode off and left me. We lived about six miles from where I worked, but I made up my mind that I would walk. I came in second and got a prize. Upon reaching home he did not open the door, so I stayed outside until he did. I tell you, when you don't have any self-esteem, you endure evil and think it's good. The situation got worse and eventually he started to get physical. I literally became his beating stick; as soon as an argument occurred, if I ever dared to answer him, he would get upset and physical. I tell you 'abuse begets abuse' and it comes in many different forms. It's worse if you are in a situation where you are drowning without a straw to hold on to; you just yield to that lifestyle as if nothing is wrong, making excuses for your aggressor. You even start thinking that you did something wrong to cause him to react the way he does. So there I was in the deep, just paddling - then to add to my sinking, his daughter from a previous relationship came to live with us. She was twelve years old at the time, additional trouble to join my household. She was what you call a 'house rat'. She would repeat our house business to one of his baby's mothers, then she would relate it back to him, like it was me telling people what was going on in our house. I was slapped with a machete, given black eyes and beaten before my daughter and his child. I just told myself I was born to suffer. I kept the abuse to myself, not even telling my best friend – I was too ashamed to do so. He called me all sorts of names and all I did was cry. Always remember; it does not matter what is happening to you - it might be long, but it won't be forever, the Lord will send someone. There was this man who came and played dominoes sometimes at the house. He said to me, "I saw Joy today" and I said "Where?" he said "At the gate". Joy is not her real name - she was one of my child's father's baby's mother. He asked if his daughter told us and I said no. That's when he said to me on more than one occasion, that he saw them at the gate and would be surprised that I did not know. He saw how I treated the child, so he didn't expect her to keep it a secret, but she knew her reasons why.

She never told any of us that she was there. That's when the father realized it was her all along that was relating our house business and I was the one getting beat for something I was completely innocent of. I could have lost my life. One night the beating was so bad, I was punched around like a bouncing ball. Something just clicked; I rushed outside and started throwing some missiles (bottles) at him. He did a lot of hopscotch that night and from that point, he never put his hands back on me. Only God saved me and I bear no grudge, I have forgiven them both. Three years later I was pregnant again. After my second child was born, I went to my aunt and she asked me if I was going to do something with my life. The place where I was working closed down a month after my child was born. There was a real bad hurricane and the company returned to the United States. I then decided I would go back to school to get a career. When I told him, he was so mad - he said I should have gone to school before I had the children. He tried to discourage me, but that did not deter me. Shortly after, I started attending cosmetology school with the assistance of my brother, who was working on a cruise ship at the time. At school I was doing well and the students couldn't understand why I was scoring 100% on most of my tests, while others were struggling. They thought I was copying, but they did not know I was always brilliant from way back - although at home, it was a different story. My children's father was mean as always; I was not allowed to study at nights, I could not turn on the lights and was not allowed to turn the television on. When he was not at home, I turned it on and made sure I turned it off before he came home. I could not use the electric iron to press my clothes - only he was allowed such privileges. I could not use the lights after I came home from school if he was awake, so I would wait until he fell asleep and turn them on. By then my youngest sister came to live with us and take care of the children while I attended school. She got a first-hand glimpse of what I was going through. I was so embarrassed. She left eventually; she could not stand it and always wondered why I put up with it. Regarding my school work, I had to put it away. Even if he was home before me, he would sit around the television and wait for me to cook dinner. By the time I finished it was bedtime and all the lights would be turned off, so I put a plan in motion.

CHAPTER 15

GOD HAS NOT FORGOTTEN

I would get up in the early hours of the morning to study. At one point my classmates thought I was cheating and brought it to the attention of the teacher. Even when I was put in the front of the class, the scores were the same. I was naturally brilliant and at the end of the 8-month course, I was first in the theory and second in the practical. I was chosen to be the valedictorian on graduation day. I was then offered my first teaching job in 1990 at the same school. I stayed with my children's father and we would argue continuously, with him telling me that I must leave his house and I would stay with my brother. By then, one of his baby's mothers was pregnant and she said it was by him, so there was no peace. We had a terrible arguement, he called me all sorts of names in the book and told me to leave. I took the children and left. He begged me to come back, but I told him to give me some time because he was always running me and each time, the same thing was happening. Within three weeks he was in a relationship with my classmate. You would think I was glad because I finally got rid of him and the abuse - but instead, I was thrown into depression. It was like I was going insane. If I knew your phone number, I would call and tell you and cry. I could not stay home and became a 'wandering dew'. I had to just keep moving and the more I heard of his carrying on, the more I was losing it. I lost a lot of weight but trust me, I was still willing to let him use me. I remember one night I went to his house with him and the girl came in the morning and called him. I went to look and when she saw me, she turned back. He locked me outside and ran after her. I was distraught that day and was hurting really bad. I went to a lady next door and cried that day like a baby. Even after that, I went up there late one night and he did not open the door. He said I kept talking and the girl was hearing about it - so I stayed outside until the morning. You think I would learn my lesson. I still went back and that's when I found out they got engaged at the airport when she was leaving for Canada. She wrote to him and I read the letter when he was asleep. He was thinking all was well and that they were going to get married and go to a foreign land, but she had a change of heart. She returned to her child's father and married him instead. I started talking to different people and nearly lost my life in the process. I was talking to two guys at the same time, but they lived eighteen miles apart - so I decided to go with the one that lived the furthest away. He had a vehicle and we were on our way, when he stopped to buy something in a shop. I was left alone in the vehicle when all of a sudden it started to move with me in it. I began to panic because I did not know what to do; I could not drive at the time and that's when I had a divine intervention from the most HIGH GOD. I heard a voice in my ear and it said stretch out your foot - I was so scared, I did not respond. The voice repeated and I did nothing, then the voice spoke with more urgency and that's when I stretched out my foot and immediately the van stopped. I was a nervous wreck when the guy came to the door. My foot was on the brake and I was trembling; he turned it off then lifted my foot off the brakes. When I got out, I saw the steep hill that I came down. I know without a shadow of a doubt, that it was the hand of God that guided my foot because there were three things down there and I didn't even look to see where my foot was going.

The enemy wanted to take me out early, but the good Lord would not allow him. The guy was telling me that as he entered the shop, the shopkeeper said to him, "You have another driver?" He said no, then the man said "Your vehicle is moving". That's when he ran behind it, but he could not catch it because of the hill. He said he panicked because he thought something bad was going to happen. But all praise and honor belongs to the Lord for saving me. After that incident I did not go back to his place, so we parted company. After a while, I started talking to a nice young man who worked with the government. He encouraged me and I began to take pride in myself. I was teaching at the school in Portland and he said I could get better wages and that the Principal at the time was not being fair. That's when I decided to look around for a different school. I saw a job in the newspaper where a school in St. Ann needed a cosmetology teacher and I applied. I got the job, so when I told my children's father I was leaving for St. Ann, he asked me to marry him. I said no and he said, "Not even for the children's sake?" I told him I would not let the children be the reason to put a ring on my finger. He called me all sorts of names but still had the nerve to ask my mother to let me come back to him, after I suffered so much. I thank God for the strength He gave me; that I could break free - so after seven years, I walked away. No matter what, after a while the enemy becomes your footstool and time always heals every wound.

I told my family I was leaving for St. Ann. Believe me, my mother and I weren't even on speaking terms. I would never leave my girl's with her anyway, so I separated the children and left them with two different sisters. I had this urgency to leave Portland and could not stay there anymore. It was as if I were being driven from my place of birth entering into a new era of my life, leaving for a destination where I had no relatives; all I knew was that I had to go.

I moved to St. Ann on September 19, 1992 and began my new job the 21st of the same month. I had a friend I attended school with and she let me stay at her place for a while, it wasn't pretty but I was grateful. I slept on her floor and sometimes when I went to sleep, the door would still be open. I did not have a choice - the pay was four times what I used to get at the first school, so I was willing to make the sacrifice. Being in a situation that wasn't comfortable, I received a call that my youngest child was crying because of her ears and belly. I had just visited the end of last month and two days after I left, the problem developed. No one saw fit to take her to the doctor; my sister said that I should come. I asked for time off and went to see what was wrong. When I got there and could see that she was in the same clothes from

Sunday and I went back on Tuesday - I just took her with me, not even thinking I had nowhere to put her. I told my girlfriend the situation and she was sympathetic. I did not take her to a doctor and she never cried after I brought her to St. Ann. I learned then - only you alone can have that tender touch for your child. I was there for two days with her and you know how things go. My friend started saying that her family and people were talking. So there was this guy I was talking to; I was not even ready for a relationship, but I could not stand to see my child up all night when she should be sleeping, because the door has to be closed before we could both lay down on the floor. I know it was done out of spite but such is life - you learn as you go along. I went to live with him and his son, but he was already taken and was leaving for a foreign land soon. I told the school that I would have to return back to Portland because where I was staying was not available anymore and I had nowhere to live. They rented an apartment for me. Trust me my life was not easy, but I never give up - I just keep on trying. Now I know it was a God-driven force that was behind me, guiding me even when I encountered obstacle after obstacle - I did not give up. I did not have a piece of furniture to put in the apartment because my stuff was in Portland, so I bought a bed and a table. It was getting close to the Christmas holidays and school would be out soon. I was still at the guy's house and took my daughter with me to make a phone call. My friend's son wanted to come with me. I told him to go to his grandmother and I left, but the little boy did not go. Instead he fell asleep on the verandah. His uncle's wife came and saw him and told his grandmother that I locked him out. When my daughter and I got home, there was a big argument; his father said I locked out his son and his grandmother was saying I could not stay there because she was not really into me - she had her daughter-in-law already. School was now on break, so I left with my child for Portland to get my older daughter. She was excited to see us. I told her that I got a house, but didn't have a bed. I bought one but didn't know if it came yet, so I would get her during Christmas. She started crying that they were beating her up, that my sister's son would hit her and when she hit him back, my sister beat her. My heart was broken, so I took her with me. I did not have a sheet-set, so I took my grandmother's table cloth. I decided that we all would sleep on the floor if the bed had not arrived. Upon our return, the bed and the table were there. I was so glad that the children would not have to sleep on the floor. I used to just work and when I got paid at the end of the month, I took what I needed and used the rest for looking after the children, but still that was not enough; nobody can care for your child like you.

I got them into school. I tried to get their father to assist, but he wouldn't. If I took six months to send them - he barely gave them their bus fare, much less food money and he was in a good position to help them. After two years at the school I was fired on the grounds of jealousy. The Principal's wife had a grudge against me; she was always comparing herself to me and she never rested until her husband fired me. I had opened a little salon without the school community knowing, so I was not left on my face. I just had to move out of the house they were paying rent for. When the students saw that I was not at school for the week and there was a new teacher who couldn't measure up to my standards - all the students came looking for me on Friday after school. I felt so proud. I remember a man in the district saying to me "You must have been a good teacher to bring one bus load of students in the district". There and then, was when they asked me to tutor them and that's when I opened my first little cosmetology school. They had already paid their fee to the school. I did not gain financially when I started but I felt self-worth, complimented by self-gratitude; to know that I grasped enough knowledge so that I could impart to others, who themselves have now established long-lasting careers. Many now work on cruise ships or own their own businesses. I am so grateful to God for giving me knowledge so that I could study a subject that covers many different career paths. There were students like myself who felt rejected; I just spoke a word of vision into their lives and they are doing well today. I remember this student, she could not read and the course entailed a lot of theory; but I knew that if I could just get her to grasp the practical, she could make something out of her life. So I worked with her and when I was finished, her parents couldn't believe it. They were so pleased, they would have done anything for me. Back then I knew the text books like the back of my hand. You would have thought I wrote them and many strived to be like me. God made me special and I know the day will come when I will have the privilege of going back to school and sit in a college or university. My latter days will be greater; my best is yet to come. It wasn't easy. I had my own rent - plus business rent to pay, children in school and family calling. I had my plate full, but I persevered. My mother came every other week and I gave her money when she was returning to Portland. I remember the first time she came to visit and we were around the table eating. I started to cry; I had to go in my bedroom to cry and finish my meal in there. I could not eat with her, everything just started flooding my memory. To this day, she doesn't know that occurred. We have to be careful how we treat our children. If you are a parent and you are doing this, cease and desist; the words of the Lord are real - Whatsoever a man sows, so shall he reap. You can't plant peas and expect to reap corn. It will come back to you some day and you are going to feel bad. I will now share something with you; I had gone to look for a church sister of mine and the Lord would have it that she told me this.

She told me that she has four children - three girls and one boy. She said she treated one of her daughters bad and ignored her through the years. She said she put the other three on top; life was good with her and money was not her problem. Then she got sick and there was no one to look after her. She said she could not believe it - especially her son whom she had invested so much into. She lost her eyesight too. Someone told her daughter and she could not believe the same rejected child showed up and was the one responsible for her well-being. I told her that God is a good God. She said she just changed her will and left everything to her. Good ending, but yours might not be like that, so make sure you do the right thing.

CHAPTER 16

AN OVERCOMER

After two years, the landlord of the place where I had the school said he wanted to renovate, so I closed the business. I could not afford the rent in the town area where I was living, so I got a one-bedroom in Steer town. I usually gave my landlord breakfast and dinner, but one day I decided to stop because he was getting his rent. That man made my life so miserable; he would turn up his music loud and I would turn up my television. When he knew I was asleep, he would call people in the house to let them listen to how loud I had my television turned up, but didn't let them know what he did. I had to take him to court. He turned off my electricity, so I moved out quickly. I did not get anywhere, so I sent the children back to Portland for a year and asked someone to store my furniture. During that year I stayed at four different places. The first place was a friend of mine's parent's house. I was there for three months when her mother said I could not stay because her biological daughter was not allowed to come there. She and her dad did not get along, so I went to another friend's house. I was there for three months when she decided she wanted her house. Another friend of mine had an apartment and I stayed there for four months. I then left and went where my things were being stored. I began apartment hunting vigorously because the children were not happy and I was getting more and more concerned. I found one about two months later, so I moved in on a Friday and retrieved my children on that Saturday. The children were so glad.

My aunt told me to leave the small one with her but I was not going to separate them, so we went back to St. Ann.

By now, the girls and I were living in Steer town again. I rented a little shop for my hair-dressing business and everything was going well. My business took a hit because of a rumor. I tell you, we can be very cruel and mean to others without realizing the grave destruction and havoc we can create. I had a student who lived in the apartment that I rented; it was her uncle's place. She came to my school and we became friends. At that time people would contact my school if they needed someone to work. This lady contacted me, so I helped her get her first job and she now works on a cruise ship. Her relatives pretty much assumed that a friendship couldn't be like that and they started telling people that we were lesbians. In my country, people are homophobic to homosexuals. They told the girl's mother how the teacher was bothering her daughter, so eventually everybody stopped coming -and if someone and I had a conversation, they would be cursed. As a result, I had to close it down. Tried as I may, I just could not convince them otherwise because it was coming from her relative's mouth, so I locked shop and moved. These things only made me stronger and my Lord always made me a cut above the rest. I might not be rich - but I always stand out. People have to marvel about me. I just forgive them and move on and let the Lord be the judge, as the psalmist David said; *He prepare a table before me, in the presence of my enemies, all who thought that I would have come to nought, have to stand aside and watch as my creator and redeemer raise me up.* I take things in stride and humble myself before Him as I continue. My oldest daughter got ill when she was about ten years old. When I took her to the doctor, they realized she had rheumatoid fever and that took a toll on me. She was admitted to the hospital quite often and missed a lot of school. The fever did not affect her heart and that itself was a blessing. The older she became, the fever was less of a threat as long as she took her injection, but that was a struggle. She was so scared of the injection; I used to send her to take it by herself. She was now in high school. Just when I thought everything was alright, I learned she was forging the nurse's signature on papers. When I found out, I rushed her to the doctor. He said since she hid it and did not take it for six months, she didn't have to take it again - but if she got a fever, I had to bring her back. Thanks be to God it gradually left her. Then the younger one had cellulitis in her knees and had to be admitted to the hospital. She was not an easy child; I had to buy her chicken and chips every day because she refused to eat the hospital food. The nurse used to say to me

"Mother, I am sorry for you". That too passed and life was okay again.

It was not nice for the girls. I did not want what happened to me to happen to them because they had step-fathers in their lives. Thanks be to GOD they were never molested. I protected those girls with my life. I never let them sleep over anyone's house - it didn't matter how close I was with the person. If I were in a relationship and the man spoke too harshly to them, he had to go. I did not allow a man to hit them and I made that clear from day one. If my child told me that the sea was black and someone else of influence told me the sea was red - I believed my child over that person. I was a disciplinarian and because of this, they had good manners. I built a good relationship with them; told them not to hide anything from me and it worked. It didn't matter how stupid it sounded - I listened to them and they developed a trust in me to this day. I remember going home in October and my youngest child said to me, "Mommy I have something to tell you", my heart started to beat. I asked her anxiously, "What is it?" She said, "Mommy you see Junior? (Junior was her cousin) Every time he sees me bathing, he just stares at me". I felt a relief and my mind started to run wild. I told her all she had to do was cover herself, then I laughed my heart out. There I was thinking it was something else. They know I would not subject them to any form of abuse. It didn't matter what you had to offer, they came first. It does not matter what a man can contribute; never subject your child to a life of abuse - men will always come and go, but your children will always remain yours. Do not destroy your children by allowing them to become bitter against you. Some will forgive you, but some won't.

CHAPTER 17

GOD'S MERCIES

I remember clearly an incident with my daughter when she was about fourteen. I was talking to this guy and he tried to tell me that my child was only pretending to be good and that once my back was turned, she misbehaved. I asked him what she was doing; he said she was giving him my birth control pills to take. When I asked her, she said it wasn't true, so I told him he was lying and that's when he got mad at me. He simply could not understand how I believed her over him and was offended. He said he was going home. When he walked through the door I went to close it, but he was still on the steps, so I did not close the door. I was going to wait until he left before I closed it and that's when I heard the voice for the second time telling me in my ears, 'close the door'. I did nothing, then the voice repeated; 'close the door, he is going to cut you up'. I still did not close it - instead I woke the children to tell them he was going to cut me up. That was when the voice shouted 'close door!' I disobeyed and that's when he rushed in with a knife, but my children jumped in the middle and I only ended up with a busted mouth. I could have lost my life and he could have pushed the knife through the children, but the Lord had a purpose for my life and He protected me again. You have people preaching garbage that the LORD doesn't talk with sinners; I was a sinner doing everything in the book you can think of. I just kicked that man out of my place; all he wanted was an opening and he would have started taking advantage of her. That's how they come in, then put you against your children. If you allow them, they will take advantage of them - but for me it will be death before dishonor. I continued to struggle with the girls on my own. I had to play the field when things got tight and would have someone paying the rent, while somebody else was buying food. For a while this was how it was, but I kept it away from the children and never stayed out all night. I was always home. I then started to manage a salon and things became much easier.

CHAPTER 18

DISASTER HITS HOME

After three years living in St. Ann my step- father got ill, which meant nothing to me. At the time, my mother would call and tell me everything that was taking place and that she was hitting him. I always discouraged it; telling her not to react that way and if she were not careful, it was going to happen to her because she always supported him with his wickedness. I will advise anyone who chooses to molest little children to defer from it, because your suffering will not be pretty. Not to rejoice in it - but to confirm that no sin goes unpunished. I will tell you all that my afflicters went through it;

especially the one that molested my two sisters and me - he suffered the most. He would lay down when he got ill like he couldn't move - but when my mother left for the market, he would get up with feces all over him and lay down in her bed to mess it up. She put him in a different room, but he would just sit on the settee and mess it up. She would wash clothes and put them on a chair; he would lift up the clothes, hide his mess under there and cover it up. When she called me raging mad I had to laugh, I could not help it. He could not eat at one point, so I gave her a blender. The dog ate two of his toes and he did not feel it; it started to smell and my sister noticed it. By the time they took him to the hospital - gangrene had already taken over most of his foot, so the doctor cut it off. He got to a point where he could not speak and shortly after, he died. I did not return once to see him. If I had known the Lord at that time I would have, so he died without me forgiving him. My step-grandfather suffered too. He was paralyzed and had real bad bed sores - but the differences was I always made sure he was taken to the doctor. I remember the last time I visited him, he could not speak. When I said to him, "Papa a me Claudette", tears ran down his cheeks. I was so moved, I cried. I never left him and had forgiven him. I was there until he passed. My uncle struggled a lot too. He was in and out of prison and he died from the dreaded disease, A.I.D.S. I contributed towards his funeral. My first step-father who started the molestation; I don't know what became of him. This is a lesson to all perpetrators; God is watching and you won't escape His judgement. Always remember that no sin goes unpunished. My mother is still alive. I confronted her in front of my grandmother and she cried. She said she did not know these things - but I reminded her that she did know, because I told her. She still told my sister that she couldn't believe I said in front of her mother - that her husband molested me. My sister told her I had to talk because I was the one feeling the pain. To tell you the truth, it was better I did not hear that. I felt like somebody stabbed me again. I was so angry to know that she was more worried about her dead husband, than me. I did not say a word to her when I was told. I was angry in the sense that she never acknowledged that it was wrong, not even to say sorry. But vengeance is for the Lord and not for me, so I would continue to support her and my grandmother as long as the Lord gave me breath. I prayed that she would surrender her life to the Lord and make peace with him. I was proud she did. I became Joseph, as the Lord said - I took the very best care of her. I made sure all of her bases were covered when it came to anything concerning her. She became ill due to her heart. When doctors diagnosed her in Portland, I had to pay for her tests and would still let her go to St. Ann to re-take the same tests. She would pray God's blessing on me. When she went in the hospital the last time, it was hard because I did not see her for the three years when she went into a coma. I was distraught knowing that I did not tell her I had forgiven her. When she came out of it, I told her I forgave her for the abuse and that I loved her because she could have aborted me. So out of evil cometh good. She passed away on November 15, 2013.

CHAPTER 19

NEW LIFE, SAME STORY

I met my first husband while I was managing a salon. Soon after, I left the salon for a teaching job at a cosmetology school. I met Noel through a mutual friend who told me he was a nice man and that he was looking for someone nice. I was not interested at the time. I was in a relationship with this guy who had a baby's mother - but after a confrontation with her, I decided to leave. He punched me when he realized I was leaving, but I took it and walked away. My friend totally convinced me that Noel was the right choice, but I was in for a rude awakening. When I assessed my situation, I said to myself - he is in a good job and I am working, so I can finally settle down and the children will be alright. Not even two months into the relationship, I realized that he was a cheater. When I went back to my friend to ask her what kind of man she gave me, she said I should take advantage of him and that she never told me to love him. This was different from what she was telling me before - so can you imagine, it was either I take it or I leave it. I decided to take it. I just told myself I could benefit from him, so I went along with his behavior. He had his place and I had mine. Sometimes I wouldn't see him for eleven days, but he always had some lies to tell. I started to push my agenda, which was to control. Not for anything but to become the center of his life and if I achieved this - I could one day marry him and get a visa off of his. That's all I wanted because I would start to travel and possibly find someone better - that was my intention. I showed up at his home without calling and once he realized what I was doing, he began sleeping at my place. His place became the brothel; that's where he did his thing before he came home.

I was still working at the school and he left for the United States of America for a month and did not call me until fifteen days afterwards. That's when I realized he was not at his daughter's as he claimed; he was with a woman, because he could not give me the number where he was staying. Anyway before he returned, on this particular day I was marking test papers. The students had already left and that's when the voice of God spoke to me. This was the third time and I was still a sinner. He told me to go down by Lewis and get a piece of the land. I turned my head to see who was speaking and I saw no one. Then He repeated – "Go by Lewis and get a piece of the land" and that's when I said, "Piece of the land?" And He answered me and said "Yes go down by

Lewis and get a piece of the land". Remember now, I am not from St. Ann but I used to live there. Anyway, I began to call around. I had gotten a piece from a guy - but when I got there, I stopped to talk to an old friend of mine and he asked me why I was taking land from that family. In the midst of talking, I heard someone say "Why don't you ask Tony?" To this day, I can't tell you who said that. I looked for Tony - meanwhile the guy said that I came to him, but I stopped talking. That's when I told him I was going to ask Tony and his comment was, how was I going to go up there? I asked him what he meant and he said, "It's the prettiest piece of land, but there is no road to get there". I still did not change my mind. I did not see Tony, so I left him a message and he sent word in the morning for me to come and choose the piece I wanted. He made sure to tell me "It's for you and the children". That's where my beautiful home is built today. When the Lord gives you something, no devil in hell can take it from you. A lot of people don't understand how I got it, but it's the Lord's doing. I have learned that once He tells you something, he will pave the way; He will move every barrier for you to achieve His accomplishment.

CHAPTER 20

ANOTHER STEP IN LIFE

So after my ex-husband returned from his journey, I told him I found a place to build a house. The children were now in high school; the sickness had taken a toll on the older one, so she did not do so well in school. The younger one was showing great promise and deep down I was glad, but could not show it. I needed a roof over my head, so when I got paid I started buying blocks and material, only to run into an obstacle. When I attempted to leave the material on the property, a lady who lived at the bottom said I could not drive on the road because it was hers. Now I realized what the guy was talking about. I had to leave the material at the end of the road and sixty-two blocks, out of two hundred and fifty were stolen. I had to save the rest and go to the land authority. God bless the counselor at the time - Mass Hugh, who stood with me and kept hope alive. Land authority intervened and that's when the road was freed up. The man that gave me the place tried for years and could not stop her from digging up the road and blocking it. He too had gone to the land authority, but nothing happened. A lot of people in the area were amazed; I was the first person to live on that property. When you look at my situation; a complete stranger, God freed up the road that was held in bondage for years. God is a good God and He makes the impossible possible. So we started to build and I began to make sacrifices. I could not afford to buy clothes again because every cent I received was put towards the house. I was still living in Steer town and Noel and I planned to get married when the house was finished. In October 2001, I went bed and had a vision where I saw a sign written before me in black and white that read; BEHOLD, I COME QUICKLY. I found myself running to my neighbor to tell her to baptize me and she said she couldn't because she was a sinner also. I left feeling dejected. As I was leaving, I saw a lady who attended the Jehovah witness movement and I said to her, "I just saw a sign" and I told her what I saw. She said she couldn't see any sign and she was speaking so loud that the crowd began to gather. All of a sudden, the writing appeared before everyone. This time the same thing was in gold; 'BEHOLD, I COME QUICKLY' in the prettiest hand-writing my eyes have ever seen. Then I noticed that everyone got quiet and they all bowed. I heard a man's voice from above saying something, but I could not hear exactly what he said, so I asked a girl what he said and she shrugged her shoulders. Then I heard the voice say 'Follow me'. I left more confused, so I went to a place I did not know and ended up sitting on a step. That's when the writing started to run before my eyes; it was like I was watching a screen. The writing read; 'I wanted to come a long time, but people like you are the reason why I can't come. I am going to take my covering from you and it's your last chance to get your house in order'. When I woke up in the morning I was a brand new person. I told everyone the vision and also that I was surrendering my life to the Lord. I used to say curse words, but He took them from me that night. I took off my jewelry and went to church that same Sunday. I would go two Sundays in a row, then break for a week so that I could repeat my clothes. I only had two suits and you know the pressure you feel these days when you attend churches; you feel like a lesser being because the brethren are so dressed up. I would advise anyone who wants to serve the Lord - go as you are, the word of God says whatever state you are in, you ought to be content and it is only a matter of time before your change comes. As a matter of fact, it is all about the heart. The good book says you are to render your heart and not your garment. One Sunday during the altar call, my friends and I were in the back talking. I told them I wasn't going to go up there because I had already surrendered and I was getting married in a few months. It didn't make sense for me to go up there every week anyway. I heard the man of God say, "You at the back", the minister at the time was Pastor Neil Morris. I turned around to see if it was my friend he was speaking to, but as I turned he said "You, the one that just turned her head". I went up with a frown on my face and that's when he said, "God forbid if I would call you up here to embarrass you", he proceeded to say, "The Lord said, if you just surrender your life to Him you will see what He has in store for you" and he sent me back to my seat. I was puzzled knowing that I had not told anyone in that church anything because I just started attending. I was there with my old friends, but later I realized it was confirmation from the Lord. I started to go more often and my sister gave me some of her used clothes. I would go and leave the children behind. I was telling this lady that I wanted to bring the girls, but I was not in a position to buy them church clothes. She told me that her granddaughter had some, so she would give them to me and that's how the children started to go. I got married in August 2002 and was baptized in December that same year.

CHAPTER 21

NEW JOURNEY

I moved to my new place of abode in September 2002. It was better than paying rent. We had finished the hall completely, but the bedroom and bathroom were only partially done, so we decided to all stay in the living room. My aunt said we should move in the bedroom and leave the children in the hall. I moved in the unfinished bedroom and was walking on the boards, because the floor was not finished yet and I got something stuck in the bottom of my foot from the stones. My friend Natalie came by to see me and when she saw me on the boards, she told me to come to her mother's shop and she would give me some cardboard to spread on the floor. It really worked and walking was easier. We had it like that for a while. We were without electricity and would light candles for a while, then sleep in the dark. My friend's mother loaned us a light and she would charge that light through her electricity every day until ours came on. When it was charged it lasted for two hours, so we continued with that. I can remember one night I woke up and it felt like someone other than us was in my room. I called the children by their names and I heard no answer; I knew they were asleep. I had gotten a lamp so that I would not have to sleep in the dark anymore, but on this particular night I woke up and the place was in darkness. I got up to light the lamp and as I struck the matches, I heard someone hissing through their teeth. I knew it was evil; it thrives on darkness, so I had a prayer meeting at the house and we were left in peace. Our bathroom and kitchen were incomplete, so we had to improvise. The children and I were in the most discomfort because my husband had different places to go, but we had nowhere else. We made our own toilet by using a bucket with a plastic bag in it. When we got tired of that, we would sit on a ladder and place newspaper on the ground to receive number 2's. I got so tired of the condition that I had to speak to my husband firmly for him to get the equipment from his job to make the pit. All the fixtures were already in. After much frustration it was done. I was still in church; the children got baptized, then my husband. We were going to church as a family, but my husband went back to his old ways.

In 2005 I got my United States visiting visa. I was still trying my best to get the house in order so that I could move the girls out of the living room. My oldest was attending H.E.A.R.T. My youngest was still in high school. I left for the states in 2006 and did not even have a pair of shoes on my feet. I had to borrow my daughter's shoes; ones that my church sister gave her. God bless America; on my return I had shoes in abundance and was able to share among friends and families. When I came back, everybody was out of church but I continued with my Lord.

The children started going to parties and I told them I wasn't opening any doors for them. They would still go, but when they returned they had to stay outside until the morning. To make matters worse, I did not have a veranda at the time, so they had to sit on the steps. I was serious. They continued for a while, but could not manage to be out in the dew. Plus I would not allow them to sleep in bed - especially on Sundays. They had to come to church - otherwise I just locked up my house until I returned from church, so they quit partying. I would laugh in my room when the phone rang and I heard them say they were locked out. I always told them to go live on their own; I would be out of order to come to their place and dictate to them what to do, but whatever I say goes in my home – they had to take it or leave it. When their bedroom was ready, they wanted a door with a lock but I gave them a curtain. I was not going to be locked out in my own house and when the Holy Spirit said to cover them, I'd have to beat down the door. I needed easy access at all times. They thought I was being harsh but as the story goes on you will see how they benefited. Children are our heritage and we should protect them - whatever you put into them, that's what you'll get. You give them a mile and they will take a yard and if you let things slip, next time they will take more yards. It was my oldest daughter's last year in high school and I promised her I would send her to their sport day. She had never been to one. My neighbor's sons were having their sport day, the children asked me if they could go and I said yes. I told them not to let six o'clock catch them and I even reminded the older one that if she stayed over the time, she could forget going to her sport the next day. When evening came I saw everybody coming but no sight of the children. Their curfew had passed and I waited patiently until they arrived. I said to them, is this six o'clock? They had all sorts of excuses. I said to my eldest, "You can forget your sport, you swapped it for theirs". She begged me and called who she could to plea on her behalf, but I did not budge. She learned her lesson and never let it happen again. There was a prank they played on me one day; I was washing clothes and I heard Marsha call me. I asked her what she wanted and she said something about the electrical cord, but I didn't pay her any mind. Then I heard a strange sound and she was calling more earnestly, so I stopped what I was doing. You should have seen me leap over that pan and run towards them with my heart pounding, thinking my child had been electrocuted - but when I reached them they started to laugh, which immediately became tears. I gave both of them the same punishment. They both said it was the other's idea, but I wasn't responsible for whose idea it was. I always told them if one did something and the other kept the secret and did not tell me, both would get in trouble and be punished equally. So I always knew what was going on – no one wanted to be punished for things they were innocent of. Those girls were something else. You should hear us when we are together and going down memory lane. They both did well and I couldn't ask for better children.

CHAPTER 22

HE BROUGHT ME THROUGH IT

I returned to the states again. Everything remained the same with the children, but my husband started staying out. He was telling our relatives that the children were telling me things. After a while, he got the message.

I was faced with a situation. There was a lady that was seen in his van all the time - but I just told myself that life is hard, so he was being kind. One day I was coming from fasting and my daughter showed me the van. While approaching the van, the Holy Spirit said to me, "He has a check". I asked him, "Do you have a check?" He said no and that's when I told him (lying in the process) "Your co-worker told me he got one" and he said "No, I won't be getting any check until December." But I knew once the Holy Spirit said it, it was true. So I said nothing more. I just told myself sometime during the night, I would search the van. That was the longest night; every time I reached the door, the voice said to me, "Turn back he is coming" and as I turned back and came around the corner, we would collide. I returned to bed and got up again, but he was up too. So when he thought he had me and everything was fine, I went in the children's room talking loud so he could hear me. Meanwhile I was making signs to my nephew; I had a spare key, so I told my nephew who was living with me, to go and look in the van - and if he saw a check, to bring it to me. I normally get up at 5.30 am to pray - so when my nephew heard me, he came and handed me the check. All I could say was, what a God. I said nothing to him. When morning light came, he left for work and I watched him.

He went to his hiding place and when he saw that the check was gone, he came back and asked me if I saw some money he left in the van. I said to him, "Did I not ask you if you had a check and you said no?" I said, "You are nothing but a cheater, no man tell me this - it was the Holy Spirit that did, that's why I knew you had it." I did not say another word, I just walked out and left him. He mumbled something and left for work. I was not going to give him any of the money, because he said he had none. I cashed it the same day and bought some much-needed things. I called him to pick me up after work. Regarding what was to transpire; he had his plan set. He was going to give his lady friend a portion of the money (if not all of it) and that's why she came to meet him.

My church sister and I were talking and I saw the van approaching. He came and I showed him the things I bought and he put them in the vehicle. I continued talking to my church sister, then she said to me "Where is your husband?" I said, "He is around the front". I went to look for him and saw him bending down, but he was looking across the road. I did not pay it any mind and sat down with my back towards him - still talking with my church sister. Then I felt somebody put their hand under my face and spin me around; there I saw my husband across the street and a lady approaching him. Then I could hear when he said 'my wife', but she did not hear him and was still coming towards him and that's when he repeated 'my wife, my wife'. It was like a scene in a movie being played out before me. She started looking around, but because she did not know me, I just stood there watching her. She put on her dark glasses and made a hasty retreat towards a taxi and sat looking nervous. I said to my church sister "You see that?" She said yes. I told her I was going to her and as I stepped off, she grabbed my hand but I snatched it away. I told her it would be alright. I went to the car and said to her, "You are the one that has been driving in my husband's van". She said she begged him for a ride, then went on to say she was married. I found myself saying to her, "Don't tell me that you are married, because people who are married, do the most despicable things and do not respect their marriage". I walked away then heard clearly in my spirit "You let in the enemy". When I heard that I knew there was more than what she told me - so I did a little investigation, only to find out that my husband was seen at her home. Can you imagine how I felt knowing that her husband was in the house when they were doing this? All the things that I endured kept coming back, the insult. I was so hurt that all kinds of thinking started coming to me. I told myself I was going to beat her and I was going to give everybody else's share to her; and that's when the enemy crept in. I went to my neighbor who was unsaved and told her everything that happened. I told her I was going to use my umbrella and beat her. She told me she had a piece of iron and that I should use it. She went to get it and brought it back in a black bag. She said that after I used it, I should throw the evidence away. The iron felt perfect in my hand; it had two bumps, one at each end and I knew I could control my grip on it. I did not sleep that night. It was the longest night and at one point, I said to the Lord; Lord I know you must be disappointed in me, but it's like I am possessed. I can't help myself - if you don't help me I am going to be destroyed. As soon as daylight came, I told my children I was leaving. My eldest child - how she cried and pleaded with me not to go. "It's the plan of the enemy", she said. I just turned away and left. I took the short cut and said to the Lord again; Lord I know that I am in trouble, but I can't help myself. I said, Lord you have to send a help. The enemy is out to destroy me and I can't help myself and I continued on my way. I hid at the place where my husband normally picked her up and was there for a while, so I thought she might not be going to work. I was still waiting and there she was coming out of a taxi. I stepped out from where I was to go towards her. As I was walking across the street - I looked up the road and saw a van that looked like my Pastor's. I looked more keenly and saw that it was Pastor, so I went back in my hiding position. He stopped at the cross road then drove off. I made my move again, only to see the van turning on the road and heading back down where he was coming from, so I retreated again. This time he came and parked right behind the lady and loosened his tie. Her skirt was touching the van - that's how close he was. I could not believe my eyes. I was still there hoping he would leave, but instead a bus came and she got on it. About ten minutes afterwards, he left. Boy I cried that morning. My in-laws were saying to me it must have been the Lord - that's why I did not get to hit her. I went home and my daughter was glad to see me. Her eyes were swollen and she cried hard. I shared everything with her and told her I was going to Pastor, because I needed to know why he was there. Two days after, I went to the man of God and told him everything. He said to me "Sister Claudette the Lord loves you". He then said with anger, "You were going to kill her". He said he had never parked there, but he was on his way to Browns town and the Holy Spirit told him to turn back and go park there. He obeyed and stayed there until he said he could leave - and that's what he did. He told me to let it go, let the Lord deal with it and that's what I did. It was not even a month afterwards when she put her husband out. Just read between the lines and see how the enemy was setting it up. I took leave from the choir for a while; it was like I was down in the valley. I used to pray to the Lord to restore my soul and gradually I got my joy back and took up my rightful place in Zion. The struggles continue, but GOD IS A GOOD GOD.

My oldest child finished her courses and got a job at Sandal's resort. My youngest child got five subjects and that brings joy to my heart knowing that she achieved what I could have if I had gotten help. She went to college to complete her Associate's degree in business administration. It was rough, but I knew I had to do everything in my power to keep her in college. I paid the first term and called her father for help. He gave me all sorts of stories; he believed when a child finished high school, that was it. It did not matter about their potential. I did not have any choice but to take him to court. The judge asked him how much he could pay and he said a thousand dollars a week. The judge granted that, but he still would not pay so I let them arrest him and he paid the money at the same time. I did it a second time and the children complained, so I left him alone. My daughter finished her Associate's degree and is now in a university finishing her bachelor's degree. She was working at the St. Ann parish council as an accountant. After two years with the parish council, the Lord gave her a dream job; she now works at Nova Scotia bank. My eldest is married - both she and her husband, (who are sweetly saved) both work on one of the Royal Caribbean cruise line ships. Thanks be to God for turning our situation around. It now becomes one big joke when you hear them sharing what I used to do to them. Those girls appreciate me very much and still live at home, married and unmarried. I am glad that the Lord blessed me so much that life will be easier for them.

When I look back, I think how I could have committed murder and been locked away in some penitentiary and how my husband would still be playing the field. I just have to thank the good Lord for answering my prayers and sending help. He had His plan for my life and He would not allow the enemy to destroy me. He took me out of the miry clay and planted my feet on a rock to stay. I am away now in the land of the unknown, where I am patiently waiting on my master to take me to my destiny. He has started a work in me and I know that He is going to finish what He started. I continue to take care of my family and sometimes the pressure is unbearable, but I rely on my source - the Lord Jesus Christ, who once told me that I would be their Joseph. Sometimes I would ask the Lord, why is it that the ones whose parents give the worse treatment, are the ones you always leave to look after them? Sometimes I would think that if I weren't poor, maybe I would be some big executive in society. Other times I'd think maybe I would be so arrogant, I would not come in contact with the man called Christ Jesus, who restored me and made me a brand new woman who is full of love and compassion. As my journey continues I pray the Lord's blessings will continue to follow me.

I pray that all who read this book, have learned something and will be blessed while doing so. To my many students; some who now teach cosmetology, the countless many who own their own businesses and those who work on a cruise ship whose life I helped to mold - many who could not pay and yet I did not turn them away, may the good LORD shine His face upon you and give you peace. Now to all mothers especially, I hope that you have grasped something out of this book and know that it does not matter what your circumstances are in life - you are to love your children. Do not show favoritism; the only man to put before them is the Lord. Talk with them, be their best friend and as the good book says - train them the way they ought to go and when they grow old, they won't depart from it. To all you step-fathers who like to prey on your step-children like vultures; remember your day of reckoning is coming. It shall creep upon you and when you think there is peace and safety – it will be sudden destruction. No sin goes unpunished and remember that the stone that the builder refused, always becomes the head corner stone. I thank all the people who have contributed to my life somewhat. May the King of Kings and Lords of Lords enlarge your territories, continuously.

To correspond with Claudette Williams please send all inquiries to

thesstonethatthebuilderrefused1@gmail.com

www.ingramcontent.com/pod-product-compliance
Lightning Source LLC
Chambersburg PA
CBHW050638160426
43194CB00010B/1726